Fact Finders®

The
Solar System
and Beyond

Robots in Space

by Christopher Forest

Consultant:
Dr. Ilia I. Roussev
Associate Astronomer
Institute for Astronomy
University of Hawaii at Manoa

CAPSTONE PRESS
a capstone imprint

Fact Finders are published by Capstone Press,
151 Good Counsel Drive, P.O. Box 669, Mankato, Minnesota 56002.
www.capstonepub.com

Books published by Capstone Press are manufactured with paper
containing at least 10 percent post-consumer waste.

Library of Congress Cataloging-in-Publication Data
Forest, Christopher.
 Robots in space / by Christopher Forest.
 p. cm.—(Fact finders. The solar system and beyond)
 Summary: "Describes robots that do work in space and robots that explore
the solar system"—Provided by publisher.
 Includes bibliographical references and index.
 ISBN 978-1-4296-6003-7 (lib. bdg.)
 ISBN 978-1-4296-7229-0 (pbk.)
 1. Space robotics—Juvenile literature. I. Title. II. Series.
 TL1097.F67 2012
 629.43—dc22   2010052352

Editorial Credits
Jennifer Besel, editor; Heidi Thompson, designer; Eric Manske, production specialist

Photo Credits
Getty Images Inc.: Science & Society Picture Library, 22; Johns Hopkins University Applied Physics
Laboratory, 23; NASA, 5, 6, 9, 11, 12, 13, 18, 19, 21, 24; NASA: JPL, cover, 1, 3, 15, 25, 27; NASA/JPL/
Cornell University/Mass Digital, 20; NASA and Michael Carrol, 17

Artistic Effects
iStockphoto: Dar Yang Yan, Nickilford

Printed in the United States of America in Stevens Point, Wisconsin.
032011   006111WZF11

Table of Contents

Chapter 1

Helpers in Space

People have studied the night sky for thousands of years. They wondered what stars were made of. They asked why comets raced across the sky. But all their studying was done with their feet on the ground.

Rockets eventually changed that. In the early 1900s, scientists developed rockets that could be sent into space. In the 1950s, scientists used those rockets to send out the first **satellites**. Then in the 1960s, the first people traveled into space.

People continue to go into space. But the solar system is huge. People can only survive in space for short amounts of time. Scientists needed help. So they invented robots to perform jobs in space. With the help of robots, the world has learned many details about our solar system.

satellite: a spacecraft that circles Earth to gather and send information

FACT: The first space robot was sent to the Moon by the former Soviet Union in 1970. It looked like a giant robot bug.

Worker Robots

Many people think of robots as machines that walk and talk. But those are Hollywood robots. Real space robots are very different. They come in many shapes and sizes. And they're built for two main purposes.

One type of robot helps astronauts complete jobs. These worker robots **launch** satellites. They help astronauts take space walks. Worker robots also move heavy equipment or make repairs in space.

launch: to send a spacecraft into space

a worker robot called Dextre

Explorer Robots

The other type of robot is built for exploring space. Robots run on batteries and solar power. They can travel for years without rest.

Scientists use three kinds of robot explorers. Probes **orbit** space bodies. They take pictures of the objects' surfaces and gases. Landers touch down on space objects. They measure chemicals in soil and do other experiments. Rovers move around on the surfaces of space bodies. They send information back to scientists about landforms and other surface features.

orbit: the path an object follows as it goes around a dwarf planet, planet, or star

Robot Explorers

	Probe	Lander	Rover
Orbits around a space body	x		
Lands on a space body		x	x
Moves itself into sunlight to recharge	x		x
Moves around the surface of a space body			x
Runs tests on the soil of a space body		x	x

Chapter 2

Worker Robots

Astronauts who travel on space shuttles take the Remote Manipulator System (RMS) with them. The RMS is a 905-pound (411-kilogram) robot arm. The arm is 50 feet (15 meters) long when fully open. It has three movable parts that work like a human shoulder, elbow, and wrist. An astronaut controls these parts from inside the space shuttle.

Astronauts use the RMS to carry and launch satellites. The RMS can help fix satellites and space telescopes too. It also helps anchor astronauts on space walks.

A larger robot arm is used on the *International Space Station (ISS)*. This robot is called the Space Station Remote Manipulator System. Astronauts use this arm to **dock** visiting space shuttles.

dock: to join two spacecraft together in space

FACT: The RMS is often called Canadarm after the country that built it. The arm on the *ISS* is called Canadarm2.

shoulder joint on the RMS

wrist joint on the RMS

elbow joint on the RMS

9

Dextre

Astronauts on the *ISS* use other robots too. One of those robots is Dextre. This two-armed robot looks a bit like the upper body of a person. The body is 12 feet (3.7 m) long. The arms are each 11 feet (3.4 m) long.

This robot helps astronauts move objects outside the *ISS*. Dextre's work cuts down on the number of space walks astronauts have to do. Using TV cameras, astronauts guide Dextre from inside the station. They attach power tools as fingers. These tools are used for tightening bolts or grasping objects. Dextre even helps replace batteries outside the station.

FACT: Dextre weighs about 3,400 pounds (1,542 kg) on Earth.

solar panel on the *International Space Station*

Dextre

Robonaut2

A robot that looks like a person was once the thing of science fiction. Now it is science fact. One of the newest robots in space is Robonaut2 (R2). This robot has a head, a body, and two five-fingered hands. R2 is designed to help astronauts work inside the *ISS*.

R2 is only 40 inches (102 centimeters) tall. It moves its arms much like a person. And it uses the same tools as people. R2 can adjust screws, change filters, and make other repairs. While it may look like a human, it doesn't have a mind of its own. It follows programmed commands.

Scientists created two R2 robots. One is on the *ISS*. The other will be used by General Motors to test new technology for cars.

Chapter 3

Explorer Robots

Some robots help astronauts in space. Others actually take the place of astronauts. Robot explorers travel where astronauts cannot yet go.

In 1977 scientists sent the *Voyager 1* and *Voyager 2* probes to visit the outer planets. These probes carried cameras and measurement tools.

Voyager 1 flew by Jupiter and Saturn. *Voyager 2* soared past Jupiter, Saturn, Uranus, and Neptune. The probes gave scientists a closer look at these planets and their moons.

The probes sent back data that showed things scientists hadn't seen before. They discovered volcanoes on Io, one of Jupiter's moons. Scientists learned that many of Saturn's rings are made of tiny ice pieces. They also discovered that Saturn's moon Titan has seas of **methane**.

methane: a liquid that falls from the clouds on Titan; on Earth methane is a gas

A *Voyager* probe—the two *Voyager* probes were identical.

The *Voyager* probes are still traveling today. They have almost left our solar system. The probes continue to send back information. Scientists wonder what details these probes will send about space outside our system.

To Jupiter Again

Scientists learned a lot from the *Voyager* probes. But those probes simply flew past planets. Scientists wanted to study Jupiter closely. They hoped to learn how this planet formed. In 1989 NASA sent the probe *Galileo* to the gas giant.

Galileo explored Jupiter and its moons. During its 14-year mission, *Galileo* took many pictures. It sent scientists information about the planet's surface and **atmosphere**. The probe also found evidence of an ocean on Jupiter's moon Europa.

Galileo carried a smaller probe with it. It launched the small probe into Jupiter's atmosphere. This probe took pictures as it plunged toward the planet. The pictures showed enormous thunderstorms in Jupiter's atmosphere. These storms are bigger than any on Earth.

atmosphere: the gases that surround a planet or star

an artist's illustration of *Galileo* near one of Jupiter's moons

FACT: *Galileo* orbited Jupiter until 2003 when it crashed into the planet.

Voyages to Venus

For centuries, scientists wondered what lay beneath Venus' cloudy atmosphere. In the 1970s, the *Pioneer Venus* probes were sent to find out. *Pioneer I* orbited Venus. It carried tools such as **radar** and temperature probes. The probe sent back information about clouds, temperatures, and Venus' surface.

artist illustration of *Pioneer I* at Venus

Pioneer II was dropped into Venus' atmosphere. It carried smaller probes that studied the temperature, pressure, and clouds. These probes gave scientists pictures of the planet's surface.

In 1989 the *Magellan* probe was launched. The probe orbited Venus and took radar images. These images allowed scientists to map 98 percent of the planet. Scientists learned that Venus is covered with volcanoes and plains of hardened lava.

radar: a tool that finds solid objects by sending out radio waves

Magellan being launched from the space shuttle *Atlantis*

Exploring Mars

Mars is fairly close to Earth. One day people might be able visit the red planet. So scientists have spent years studying Mars.

artist illustration of a rover on Mars

In 2004 NASA sent two rovers to the red planet. *Spirit* and *Opportunity* are still on Mars today. These robots were designed to study the history of water on Mars. Scientists wonder if the planet was ever wet enough for life-forms. The rovers send information to Earth about Mars' surface.

The rovers use solar power during the day and electric power at night. They also keep track of their temperatures. They shut down when it is too cold. Powering down helps *Spirit* and *Opportunity* survive the cold Martian temperatures.

In 2007 NASA sent the *Mars Phoenix Lander* to Mars' northern pole. Scientists had studied pictures of the planet taken by satellites. They believed water might lie under Mars' poles. There, the lander's robot arm dug into the soil and found water in the form of ice.

artist illustration of *Mars Phoenix Lander* on Mars

To Mercury

In 1973 scientists sent *Mariner 10* to the closest planet to the Sun. Scientists wanted to know how Mercury survives being a neighbor to a star. The probe flew by the planet three times. It measured Mercury's **magnetic field** and temperature. *Mariner 10* also photographed 45 percent of the planet. Mercury appeared as a crater-filled planet with cliffs and ridges.

magnetic field: the space near a magnetic body where magnetic forces are detected

artist illustration of *Mariner 10*

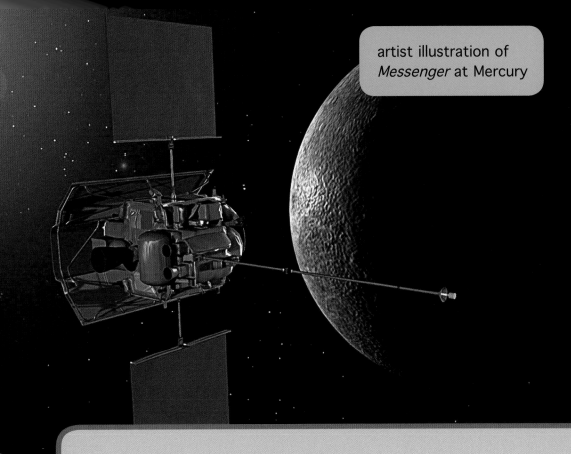

artist illustration of *Messenger* at Mercury

Mariner 10 answered some questions about Mercury. But scientists wanted to learn more about the planet's core. They also hoped to learn why permanent shadows appear at its poles. In 2004 NASA launched the *Messenger* probe. The probe began orbiting Mercury in 2011. Scientists are still gathering information to answer their questions. But on the way there, *Messenger* took pictures of areas on Mercury never viewed before.

Around the Solar System

Space robots aren't just for planet exploration. They're also used to study other space bodies. The *Ulysses* probe was sent to explore the Sun in 1990. The probe helped prove that the Sun's magnetic pole flips every 11 years. This flip means the Sun's north pole becomes the south pole.

In 1996 the *NEAR Shoemaker* probe was sent to study the asteroid Eros. In 2000 the probe began orbiting Eros. It allowed scientists to study the asteroid's surface. A year later, *NEAR* landed on the asteroid. It sent back several pictures before its communication system shut down.

artist illustration of *NEAR* at Eros

In 2004 the *Stardust* probe reached the comet Wild 2. *Stardust* gathered comet **particles**. The probe returned to Earth with the first deep space comet particles scientists have ever studied. They believe parts of the comet formed near the Sun 4.5 billion years ago.

particle: a tiny piece of something

artist illustration of *Stardust* collecting comet samples

Chapter 4

The Future of Space Robots

Scientists have big plans for new space robots. Even as you read this, probes are streaking across space.

In 2011 the *Dawn* space probe began orbiting the asteroid Vesta. In 2014 it will arrive at the dwarf planet Ceres. The probe will provide the first up close view of any dwarf planet. Scientists want to study Vesta and Ceres because they are in the asteroid belt. Material in the asteroid belt formed when the solar system was young. The probe may uncover information about how the solar system formed.

FACT: *Dawn* is named for its mission. Scientists hope it will find information about the "dawn" of the solar system.

The *New Horizons* probe is traveling to Pluto. It will be the first probe to study this dwarf planet and its moons. It should arrive at the icy world in 2015.

In 2016 a probe named *Juno* will arrive at Jupiter. It will study Jupiter's atmosphere and magnetic field.

artist illustration of *Dawn* in the asteroid belt

To Moons and Beyond

Different kinds of explorer robots might one day travel through space. Some scientists hope to send robot submarines to Jupiter's moon Europa. Europa has oceans that might be like Earth's.

Other scientists hope to send a **blimp** to Saturn's moon Titan. The atmosphere on Titan is **denser** than Earth's atmosphere. A blimp could travel with heavy equipment easily in the dense atmosphere.

Space robots have changed our view of the solar system. Who knows what mysteries may be unlocked by future space robots?

blimp: a ship without a rigid frame, much like a balloon

dense: thick or crowded

Planet Exploration

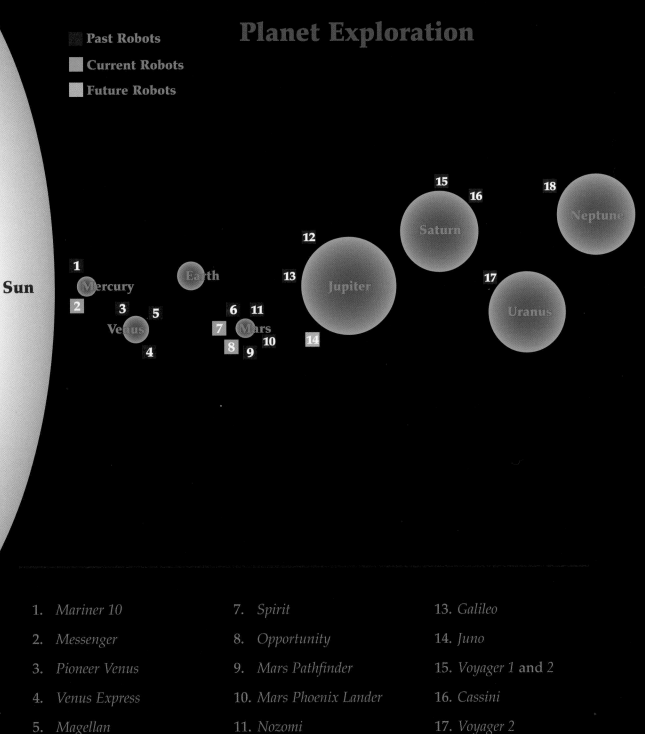

- Past Robots
- Current Robots
- Future Robots

Sun

1
2
Mercury
3
5
Venus
4

Earth

6 11
7 Mars
8 10
9

12
13
Jupiter
14

15
16
Saturn

18
Neptune

17
Uranus

1. *Mariner 10*

2. *Messenger*

3. *Pioneer Venus*

4. *Venus Express*

5. *Magellan*

6. *Viking 1* and *2*

7. *Spirit*

8. *Opportunity*

9. *Mars Pathfinder*

10. *Mars Phoenix Lander*

11. *Nozomi*

12. *Voyager 1* and *2*

13. *Galileo*

14. *Juno*

15. *Voyager 1* and *2*

16. *Cassini*

17. *Voyager 2*

18. *Voyager 2*

Glossary

atmosphere (AT-muh-sfeer)—the layer of gases that surrounds some dwarf planets, moons, planets, and stars

blimp (BLIMP)— a ship without a rigid frame, much like a balloon

dense (DENSS)—thick or crowded

dock (DAHK)—to join two spacecraft together in space

launch (LAWNCH)—to send a rocket or spacecraft into space

magnetic field (mag-NE-tik FEELD)—the space near a magnetic body or current-carrying body in which magnetic forces can be detected

methane (METH-ane)—a liquid that falls from the clouds on Titan; on Earth, methane is a gas; the cold temperatures on Titan turn methane into liquid

orbit (OR-bit)—the path an object follows as it goes around an asteroid, dwarf planet, planet, or star

particle (PAR-tuh-kuhl)—a tiny piece of something

radar (RAY-dar)—a tool that finds solid objects by sending out radio waves; space probes use radar to map a planet's surface

satellite (SAT-uh-lite)—a spacecraft that circles Earth; satellites gather and send information

Read More

Baker, David and Heather Kissock. *Probing Space.* Exploring Space. New York: Weigl, 2010.

Gross, Miriam J. *All about Space Missions.* New York: Rosen Pub. Group's PowerKids Press, 2009.

Jefferis, David. *Space Probes: Exploring Beyond Earth.* Exploring Our Solar System. New York: Crabtree Pub., 2009.

Internet Sites

FactHound offers a safe, fun way to find Internet sites related to this book. All of the sites on FactHound have been researched by our staff.

Here's all you do:

Visit *www.facthound.com*

Type in this code: 9781429660037

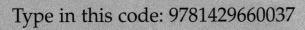

Super-cool stuff!

Check out projects, games and lots more at
www.capstonekids.com

Index